A STEP BY STEP BOOK ABOUT
LOVEBIRDS

ARNOLD WESTON

Photographers and artists: Dr. Herbert R. Axelrod, S. Bischoff, Michael Gilroy, P. Kwast, R. and V. Moat, Eric Peake, H. Reinhard, Mervin F. Roberts, Vincent Serbin, Louise Van der Meid, Vogelpark Walsrode, Dr. M.M. Vriends.

Humorous Illustrations by Andrew Prendimann

Distributed in the UNITED STATES by T.F.H. Publications, Inc., One T.F.H. Plaza, Neptune City, NJ 07753; in CANADA to the Pet Trade by H & L Pet Supplies Inc., 27 Kingston Crescent, Kitchener, Ontario N2B 2T6; Rolf C. Hagen Ltd., 3225 Sartelon Street, Montreal 382 Quebec; in CANADA to the Book Trade by Macmillan of Canada (A Division of Canada Publishing Corporation), 164 Commander Boulevard, Agincourt, Ontario M1S 3C7; in ENGLAND by T.F.H. Publications Limited, Cliveden House/Priors Way/-Bray, Maidenhead, Berkshire SL6 2HP, England; in AUSTRALIA AND THE SOUTH PACIFIC by T.F.H. (Australia) Pty. Ltd., Box 149, Brookvale 2100 N.S.W., Australia; in NEW ZEALAND by Ross Haines & Son, Ltd., 18 Monmouth Street, Grey Lynn, Auckland 2, New Zealand; in SINGAPORE AND MALAYSIA by MPH Distributors (S) Pte., Ltd., 601 Sims Drive, #03/07/21, Singapore 1438; in the PHILIPPINES by Bio-Research, 5 Lippay Street, San Lorenzo Village, Makati Rizal; in SOUTH AFRICA by Multipet Pty. Ltd., 30 Turners Avenue, Durban 4001. Published by T.F.H. Publications, Inc. Manufactured in the United States of America by T.F.H. Publications, Inc.

CONTENTS

Introduction

The petite pocket parrots known as Lovebirds are great pets for today's active people. Compact, quiet, and easy to care for, Lovebirds add a touch of active color to any home without adding a great deal of extra work. Hand-fed babies, in particular, make desirable, loyal pets for those who like the spunk and playfulness of the parrot but don't have the space or the eardrums for a larger species.

The nine species of genus *Agapornis*, the scientific name for the Lovebird group, come from the drier regions of Africa. Because they evolved to fit into a relatively harsh environment, they are hardier and more adaptable than tropical rain forest birds. Consequently, they proved quick to settle down, thrive, and reproduce when taken into captivity. Nowadays, you can easily locate many pet stores and breeders who can sell you healthy, happy birds that were bred right here at home.

We may as well mention some of the myths you've heard. In the past, the Lovebird personality was widely misunderstood. Aggressive, intelligent, and somewhat clannish, an adult Lovebird who has lived with other birds all its life won't suddenly switch its loyalties because some human offers it a treat or two. As a result, many people believed that Lovebirds couldn't be tamed or trained. Actually, the reverse is true. Once you've won over that amazingly determined spirit, Lovebirds can far surpass other small parrots like Budgerigars in their ability to learn tricks and show affection. They are so talented that

FACING PAGE:
A Peach-faced Lovebird in hiding. Lovebirds are intelligent, loyal birds who make wonderful pets if they are tamed and treated properly. The younger the Lovebird is when acquired as a pet, the easier the training will be.

a 1947 Academy Award winning film, *Bill and Coo*, featured Lovebird stars who performed their stunts and tricks for the camera even though they were fully flighted and could have flown away instead!

However, be aware that attempting to train an adult Lovebird is no job for a beginner who has other things to do. (*Bill and Coo*'s trainer had a lot of time to work with his birds because he was confined to his bed.) Fortunately, you can get the same Lovebird smarts and personality by obtaining a very

A quartet of fully colored Peach-faced Lovebirds. If you do not have adequate time for your pet Lovebird, you may wish to purchase two. The birds can then entertain each other and their owner at the same time.

An adorable Masked Lovebird. If you plan to acquire two or more Lovebirds, be sure that they are of the same or of compatible species.

young bird or even one fed as a baby by humans. Since these youngsters have learned to offer their fierce loyalties to humans from the very beginning, you can easily teach them to become the parrot pets of your dreams.

What if you don't have time to play with a parrot yourself but still want the color and amusing activity in your life? Again, the Lovebirds are just right. Get two instead of one and watch them live up to their name as they share their strong affection with each other. Either way, you're sure to join the thousands who truly love their Lovebirds.

Choosing Lovebirds

Before your buy a Lovebird or two, ask yourself what you expect of the new pet. Are you looking for companionship and perhaps the ability of the bird to learn a trick or two? Would you prefer birds that can entertain themselves when you must be away during the day? Or do you really want to try to breed the birds for show or sale? Whatever you decide, you will make better choices if you know what you're looking for in the first place.

If you want an affectionate, easy-to-train pet, give first choice to Lovebirds that have been hand-fed from an early age by humans. These birds will be more expensive because of the human labor involved, but you'll find them well worth the extra cost. A Lovebird removed from the nest before its eyes have opened will think it's a small person and behave accordingly. These inquisitive, active little birds are gentle enough to play with children, and some hand-feeders now say that such Lovebirds make better child's pets than Budgies since their sturdy bodies can take clumsier handling.

Young Lovebirds that have just been weaned are second choice for pets. With a bit of training, these youngsters can also make wonderfully loyal companions. For best results, choose a youngster under three months old. Lovebirds, like almost all birds, are plainer as juveniles, so the dull, "unfinished" looking specimens are probably younger than the beautifully turned out "peachies." If the young Lovebird's beak still has

FACING PAGE:
Two Peach-faced Lovebirds. When selecting a pet Lovebird, be sure to choose a bird that has bright plumage, good weight, and an interest in its surroundings.

black on it, you have a great candidate for pet training.

If you really don't have time to play with your birds, get a pair so that they will be able to entertain themselves. Since most older Lovebirds are hard to train as tame companions, they're usually offered in compatible pairs. However, be sure that a pair is what you want, because you'll find it difficult, if not impossible, to tame them down if you change your mind later.

Also, don't be fooled by the word "compatible." All that means is that the Lovebirds get along. It doesn't imply that they are boy and girl. Maybe they are and maybe they aren't. There's quite a good chance that they're merely close friends.

If you want to try breeding, then, you have some work ahead of you. The sexes in the most commonly available Lovebirds look alike at all ages, and young birds are particularly hard to sex. If you know someone who is experienced in handling birds, he or she can often sex adult Lovebirds by feeling the pelvis, since the bones in the female are farther apart to allow her to pass the eggs. However, a beginner has trouble with this method: your fingers aren't sure yet how far is far enough to class the bird as female. To a certain extent, you'll probably have to rely on the honesty and helpfulness of the seller.

In any case, it can be difficult to locate someone who will sell you a true pair of breeding Lovebirds. Why get rid of a proven pair that's cheap to keep and produces in-demand babies? In the long run, you will probably do better by buying several younger, unsexed birds, letting them mature, and pairing them off yourself.

You can buy Lovebirds from a pet shop or breeder. Whatever the size of the seller's establishment, it should look clean and well-maintained. Ask yourself some key questions when deciding whether you can buy a healthy bird from this person: Are the perches, seed cups, and drinkers reasonably clean? Does the bottom of the cage look like it has been cleaned in the last twenty-four hours? Are birds and cages scent-free? Lovebirds, like all parrots, are naturally clean and neat. If they have an odor, the seller isn't caring for them properly—and they probably won't be healthy enough to withstand the stress of adapting to a new home.

A congregation of Lovebirds. Since there may be several Lovebird species and color mutations from which to choose, it may be a good idea to familiarize yourself with the variations before you go bird shopping.

Before purchasing your lovebird, go to the pet store first to buy its cage. No bird should have to spend hours or even days in a small cardboard box while you shop for its home. Always buy the strongest, healthiest-looking Lovebird that you can. It's very unwise to buy pitiful, sneezing, feather-plucked little birds out of pity. You run the risk of bringing

home a disease that could infect your other pets or even yourself—and the stress of adapting to a new environment is much more likely to kill the sick bird than to save it. Sellers have a better chance of nursing their birds back to health than you do, so let them get on with it.

Depending on its degree of tameness, the Lovebird may react to your inspection by scampering away or running up for a head-scratching. Either reaction suggests a healthy bird that notices what's going on in the world around it. A sick bird, by contrast, is often too weak to care. If it doesn't even bother to open its eyes when you speak, it's probably not feeling well enough to make your acquaintance. True, most birds siesta in the middle of the day, but even a beginner can usually distinguish between a semi-alert doze and a near-coma!

Ask the seller to catch the bird for your inspection before you make a final decision. Is the keelbone, the supportive bone that runs down the length of the chest, padded by enough reserve fat to let a pouting bird do without food for a few hours? Of course, you aren't planning to starve your pet, but it does happen that a bird doesn't settle down enough to

When you approach the Lovebird cage, some birds will react by running away, and others may come right up to you. These reactions are normal and healthy, as they both show that the birds are aware of the world around them.

eat for several hours after arriving in its new home. A Lovebird with a keelbone as sharp as a knife is much too underweight to deal with any additional stress.

You should also make a visual inspection of the prospective pet. Does it have reasonably neat plumage for its age? Are its beak, eyes, and vent clean and free of any discharge? Are its eyes bright and responsive? If untame, is it reasonably upset about being captured and held? (You're unlikely to have found the world's only naturally good-natured Lovebird, you know. More likely, an untame Lovebird that seems indifferent to handling is just too sick to care.) It's true that some untame birds that are otherwise healthy may soil themselves in fear of being caught. However, since you don't know for sure why the vent is dirty, I find it best to simply request another bird.

To protect yourself and your new pet, you'll probably want to have a vet inspect your Lovebird within a few days after you take it home. If the vet finds a problem, most sellers will replace the bird. However, every seller has his or her own policies, and it's best to get them in writing at the time of sale in order to avoid any misunderstanding.

One final precaution: people who already own their birds should always keep captive-bred Lovebirds in a separate room for two full weeks. Imports should be kept separate from the others for a full month. That way, if your new acquisitions do turn out to have a disease, you won't have exposed your healthy pets.

However, don't get the idea that Lovebirds are sickly, finicky pets. Quite the contrary. They are one of the sturdiest, healthiest birds around. Despite their small size, they have lived for fifteen years or even longer. Like a cat or a dog, a Lovebird is a long-term responsibility—and a long-term source of love and enjoyment.

Your Lovebird's Home

What kind of cage should you give your Lovebird? That depends, again, upon whether your bird is a single tame pet, half of a playful pair, or part of a breeding colony. A tame pet that spends most of its day on a shoulder or in a parrot playpen will obviously require less elaborate quarters than a pair of birds who never leave their cage.

The more time you can give your Lovebird out of its cage, the smaller its cage need be. You can get away with a simple one-foot cube *if* your Lovebird spends most of the day elsewhere. If you can allow it out only in the evenings, make the cage bigger so it can accommodate some toys. These active, intelligent birds can't be expected to sit quietly in a cage that doesn't allow them to stretch their wings. Give them space to explore and exercise while you are gone.

When choosing a cage, keep in mind that a Lovebird is a parrot with a parrot's powerful beak. Its home shouldn't have plastic anywhere its beak can reach. Remember also that antique and decorator cages were often designed by people who knew nothing about birds. Tiny curved cages that deny the Lovebird the chance to climb or move around are cruel. Save these cages for protecting your ceramic birds from your Lovebird's jealous beak!

If you are handy, you can build a nice cage with clips and welded wire. You can make the larger cage sturdier by building a frame out of metal, wood, or PVC pipe. To prevent a curious beak from nibbling on a poison, avoid "pressed" or

FACING PAGE:
A pair of Masked Lovebirds. Lovebirds must be housed in a cage or aviary that allows sufficient room for exercise for each and every bird.

other chemically treated woods. You can make it easier to see into your homemade cage by painting the welded wire matte black; however, the birds are sure to chew on the paint, so make certain to use a lead-free variety. Really, you're much better off buying a cage than trying to make one. In addition to having a safer home for your bird, you'll probably save money as well.

The pair of Lovebirds that you don't intend to breed probably needs a roomier cage than a breeding pair and certainly needs more room than a single pet. You should plan on supplying a minimum of four cubic feet of space—more if you possibly can. Lovebirds do have definite personalities and opinions, and you don't want your little emblems of love suddenly jumping all over each other's nerves. Give them enough room to climb, play, and use their toys separately or together, and a compatible pair should stay that way.

All Lovebirds, even single pets, should have nestboxes

A pair of Peach-faced Lovebirds. These birds are members of the Golden Cherry, or Japanese Yellow, mutation.

A group of Peach-faced Lovebirds housed in an aviary. These birds belong to several of the different Peach-faced varieties.

attached to their cages. They will feel more secure and stay cozy at night if they have a special place to sleep. A Budgie nest- box is fine for the individual pet or a snug pair of friends, although you'll want to choose something a bit larger for a pair that you plan to breed. Since nestboxes do become soiled, plan to remove them for cleaning every two weeks to once a month when the birds aren't breeding. Thoroughly wash and dry a breeding pair's nestbox after each clutch is fledged.

Choose with care the place where your new pet will live. Even the hardy Lovebird can't be expected to stay healthy

A pair of Masked Lovebirds. Lovebird cages must contain enough good quality perches for each bird.

if a draft blows on it all night and odors assault its respiratory system all day. Because the kitchen is constantly heating up and cooling down, generating all sorts of odors and temperature differences, it's generally the worst place in the house for a bird. A quiet niche in the den or family room is usually safer, and it gives the Lovebird a great vantage point for enjoying the family's activities. Expect a squeal when you cut off its favorite TV show!

To make sure a particular location is draft-free, you can light a small candle and set it down where the cage will be. Is the flame standing tall, or is it fluttering and gusting? What happens when you open or close that door you walk through thirty times a day?

Never ask a Lovebird to share its cage with a member of another species. Occasionally, it may happen that two birds left alone during the day in nearby cages will start flirting with one another. If the Lovebird is passing food to your conure or vice versa, OK. Let them play together or even share a cage. However, the reason such stories are news is because they almost never happen. The flip side of Lovebird loyalty to its human or its mate is a fierce aggressiveness toward outsiders. A bird retailer once told me that a single Lovebird could wipe out a whole cage of mynah birds in one night. Maybe she's wrong, but I wouldn't care to put it to the test with my birds.

For that matter, don't put three or more Lovebirds in your cage. Two at a time, please, unless they're caring for their own young. If you wish to keep or breed a colony of Lovebirds,

An American Pied Light Green bird. This is a variety of the Peach-faced Lovebird.

you will need a generous flight cage or perhaps even an outdoor aviary.

The most commonly kept species of Lovebirds, the Peach-faced Lovebird and the species with white eyerings, breed in colonies in the wild, so they're great candidates for colony breeding in your aviary. In reasonably nice climates, these hardy birds can be kept outdoors year 'round if plenty of nestboxes are supplied to keep them snug and warm while sleeping.

The advantages of keeping your Lovebirds outdoors are many. The birds will exercise more and enjoy the health benefits of free exposure to sunshine. Since you have to care for only one big flight rather than several small cages, you'll have more time to simply enjoy the beauty the birds add to your yard and garden.

However, you'll need to do some careful planning to keep your aviary trouble-free. If you live in a city or suburb, you'll need to check local zoning laws to make sure that it's OK to construct an aviary in your yard. Wherever you live, you'll also need to consider installing some kind of security system to prevent predators, thieves, and vandals from getting at your birds. Finally, design the aviary to incorporate a covered shelter so that your Lovebirds can escape the heat of the day, rain or any other severe weather.

Your aviary Lovebirds will get plenty of exercise, but you'll need to furnish your indoor birds with some special toys and tools to encourage them to work out their minds and bodies. Few birds can resist a swing, so be sure to include one in each cage of nonbreeding Lovebirds. Other toys should be selected with sturdiness and entertainment value in mind. Simple wooden toys like ladders are often the best for encouraging Lovebirds to climb, chew, and explore. Some people offer bird toys with plastic parts to Lovebirds with great success, but I prefer to reserve these less sturdy playthings for finches and Budgies. In any case, never offer anything flimsy that could break into sharp pieces under the force of a determined beak.

Get or make a small parrot playpen for your tame Lovebird. These simple, open structures complete with perch, ladder, and a toy or two can be easily carried from room to

A pair of Peach-faced Lovebirds. Perches help Lovebirds keep their feet in shape. Therefore, it is a good idea to offer your birds perches of different diameters.

room so that you can supervise your Lovebird's play while carrying on with your chores. (However, don't bring the bird into a room where you're cleaning with ammonia or working with other strong chemicals.) The playpen is indispensable when you want to be with your bird but would prefer it not "help" you by shredding the bills or removing the stoppers from your ink pens.

In addition to a nestbox and a toy, every cage should be furnished with perches and "bird protectors." The latter is a protective disc of insecticide that should be hung outside the Lovebird's cage to prevent mites from taking up residence in your bird's feathers. You can easily find these discs in pet stores, so be sure to replace them at the recommended intervals.

Don't accept just any old perch that happens to come with your Lovebird's cage. Remember that the health of a bird's feet can determine the health of a bird, since a bird with hurting feet can't lie down for a rest! You might as well throw away any plastic perches that came with the cage. Your Lovebird needs wooden perches to keep its feet pads comfortable and its toenails worn down. Make sure that the perch you choose is big enough to prevent the bird's toes from wrapping around one another but not so big that the bird can't wrap its toes three-quarters or one-half of the way around it. If you have room for more than one perch, it's a good idea to choose two that are slightly different so that the bird can rest its feet by sitting different ways.

You can use natural branches from nonpoisonous trees that you know haven't been sprayed in several years. A green branch from an unsprayed apple, birch, or willow tree is a toy, perch, and vitamin supplement all rolled up into one pretty package.

Even though you'll supply excellent perches and opportunities for exercise, your Lovebird will probably need its nails trimmed from time to time. Don't delay once you notice an overgrown nail. It isn't just a cosmetic problem: the nail could snag on a toy or cage-bar joint and the bird could hurt itself trying to get free. If you like, you can get your local pet shop or groomer to do the job for a small fee. You can also take care of it yourself.

Before you start, set out your equipment. You'll need a pair of nail trimmers of the type usually marketed for puppies, a clean towel, a damp face cloth, a styptic powder or pencil, and a partner. Catch the bird in the towel, holding it gently with a hand around its back and wings to prevent it from flapping so violently that it injures itself. Place your thumb on one cheek and your forefinger on the other to keep its head still. Let it settle down a bit. Pretty soon it will probably start chewing on the towel draped loosely over its head.

Once you're experienced, you'll be able to hold the bird in one hand and trim its nails with the other, but for now, let your partner do the trimming. It's better to take off too little than too much, since repeating the job in another week is less

Your Lovebird's Home

A trio of Peach-faced Lovebirds. When setting up the Lovebird's cage or aviary, be sure that it does not become too crowded with toys and furnishings.

traumatic than cutting into the vein. However, don't panic if you do draw blood. Quickly dab some styptic powder on the moist face cloth and hold it against the bird's toe until the bleeding stops—usually a matter of seconds with this powerful combination of powder and direct pressure.

Must you cover your Lovebird cages at night? If you've situated your bird's cage wisely, probably not. However, covers can be a great way to let a bird know it's time to rest—and to discourage late-night visitors from disturbing your pet. Since birds are creatures of habit, establish a routine either way. Don't cover the bird one night and leave it sitting up wondering why it's uncovered the next.

It really isn't hard to keep a Lovebird cage neat and clean. Change the papers at the bottom of the cage every day. You should also clean the food and water dishes every day. Once a week, or more if the cage is visibly soiled, wipe down the cage with warm water and scrape the perches with sandpaper or with the special perch scrapers sold in pet stores. Don't forget to scrape or wipe soiled toys at the same time.

How you bathe your Lovebirds depends on the individual bird. Some birds like being sprayed lightly with a plant mister. Others prefer to splash in a bird bath or dog dish full of clean water placed on the bottom of their cage. You'll soon learn for yourself whether your bird prefers a bath or a shower.

Feeding the commonly kept Lovebird is easy. These hardy hookbills like a seed-based diet that's cheap, easy to store, and convenient to feed. Although some of the rare Lovebirds are pickier woodland birds, the most popular species originated in fairly dry grassland areas where seeding grasses form

Feeding

the basis of their natural diet. Moreover, most Lovebirds available to beginners will be captive bred and, consequently, used to eating easily available foods.

Any small parrot mix, perhaps mixed with a small proportion of sunflower seed, is fine. Some people offer Cockatiel mix, while others prefer to supply Budgie or even finch mix. As far as the Lovebird's concerned, one good quality seed mix is much the same as another.

That word "quality" is an important caveat, of course! Since seed loses nutritional value as it ages, you should avoid offering old, dusty, or moldy seed. An insect or two is a great source of protein, but a whole colony of bugs is probably a sign that the seed wasn't kept very clean.

To make sure nice-looking seed hasn't quietly gone stale, sprout a teaspoonful or two of it from time to time. (You can buy seed sprouters complete with instructions at any health food store.) If the seed doesn't sprout, it's too old. If it does, offer the healthy young greens to your Lovebirds.

Seed alone, however, isn't really enough to keep your Lovebird in topnotch shape. Although determined pairs of these hardy birds have been known to rear young on a diet of seed and water, this menu is hardly a recipe for health. Like any other animals, Lovebirds require a variety of nutrients including

FACING PAGE:
Two Peach-faced Lovebirds, a Cinnamon Slate
and a Cinnamon Blue. A good, varied diet will
keep your Lovebird healthy and happy
throughout its life.

protein, fat, carbohydrate, vitamins, and minerals in order to stay in peak condition.

Seeds are great when it comes to supplying carbohydrates and fats, the energy foods that the body runs on. Carbohydrate is an easily digested form of energy that a bird's body can use quickly, without much need for prolonged processing. Fats are heavily concentrated energy that can be easily stored in the bird's body for future use. They also help supply the preen gland with the oil it needs to keep the feathers sleek and shiny. Because captive birds, who don't have to fly far and wide, should store most of their fat in the cupboard instead of on their bodies, most seed mixes emphasize high-carbohydrate, low-fat seeds. Offer the higher fat seeds found in "condition-

If you keep more than one Lovebird, be sure to provide enough food for all birds. In addition, be sure that no birds are bullied by more aggressive cagemates when feeding time comes around.

Feeding Your Lovebirds

A Masked Lovebird chewing on grass. Grass, seed, and greens are all important parts of the Lovebird diet. Try to make your pet's diet as well-balanced as possible.

ing" mixes when the bird seems weak or in poor feather.

It's difficult to supply adequate protein, the substance required for growth and cell repair, from seeds alone. Since young, breeding, sick, or injured birds all require lots of protein, these birds are unlikely to thrive on a pure seed diet. It's difficult enough to see that a mature, healthy animal gets enough protein from all-vegetable sources!

Also, seeds rarely supply all of the vitamins and minerals a bird needs to use its food efficiently. Although its body can make its own vitamin C and some of the B vitamins, it must be fed vitamins A, D, and E on a regular basis in order to stay fertile and healthy. Of the minerals, calcium is most crucial because it's used to form healthy bones and eggs. If, for example, a laying hen doesn't get enough calcium or the vitamins needed to use it, her body will steal from bones and vital organs what she needs to form her eggs—sometimes with fatal results.

However, there's no need to turn into some avian version of a food faddist in order to make sure your Lovebirds are eating right. A balanced diet, based on variety, is really easier to give than to describe.

To begin with, here's an easy way to protect your Lovebirds against vitamin A and D deficiency, said to be among the biggest causes of disease among cage-birds. Get at your pet store some vitamin A and D supplement made from fish or other animal sources. Pet shops sell various types and brands of vitamin supplements. Stir in one-half to one teaspoon of the vitamin liquid per pound of seed. Let the seed soak up the vitamin mix for twenty-four hours. And there you have it—a vitamin-enriched seed that fights your bird's likeliest deficiencies. To prevent the mix from spoiling, make up small quantities.

Incidentally, vitamin D is the so-called sunshine vitamin that's formed by the bird's skin in the sun. If your bird lives in an outdoor aviary, it probably gets all the vitamin D it needs. If not, you can increase its supply of vitamin D by adding full spectrum (not broad spectrum) fluorescent lights to the Lovebird flight or bird room. Marketed under a variety of brand names, full spectrum bulbs will stress the fact that they mimic the wavelengths found in sunlight— including some that aren't visible to the eye. Sometimes, if you're buying your fluorescent tubes in an office supply shop, the literature or sales person will stress the fact that these bulbs make it easier to read or evaluate colors. Do not confuse them with broad spectrum "grow lights" that spur plant growth but really don't contain all the wavelengths required by animals.

The traditional additions to a Lovebird's diet are greens, a bit of apple every few days, grit, and a mineral block or cuttlebone. Always keep a mineral block or cuttlebone in your Lovebird's cage, replacing the old one promptly when it becomes used up or soiled. Don't get disgusted because the bird goes for weeks without touching it. You just can't predict ahead of time when it will feel the need for some extra calcium and devour the block like it's a favorite cookie.

Why offer grit, something that's obviously not much more than classy crushed rocks? Actually, there are two good reasons. One is that, since birds don't have teeth to chew with,

Healthy Lovebirds receive a diet that is rich in vitamins and minerals. It may be a good idea to consult your veterinarian or pet store owner about your pet's diet.

they need to swallow a bit of grit from time to time to help grind up the food in their stomachs. The second is that grit can also provide a source of essential minerals.

However, you have to be careful with grit. It's a sometime thing that doesn't have to be in front of the bird at all hours, or even every day. Since stressed or sick birds have been known to gorge on grit until they died, always remove the grit cup if your Lovebird seems out of shape or if you've just clipped its nails or moved its cage. You can replace it once things have returned to normal.

Greens and apples offered every other day or twice a week represent a token attempt to make sure that the Lovebird gets enough vitamins and fiber. These foods are great, but they're not quite enough to make the standard diet complete. Most strikingly, we still haven't added a good source of protein or the calcium often found along with it.

Fortunately, it's easy to add protein to a Lovebird's diet. You don't have to do anything esoteric like stalk wild insects or mix strange formulas. One very simple way to offer protein is to get some game bird or turkey starter from a feed store. These scientifically formulated foods contain vitamins A and D in addition to protein and calcium. (Chicken starter does too, but you shouldn't offer it to your Lovebirds because it often contains medications that are bad for pet birds.) If you live in an urban area and can't get to a feed store, you can try dried dog food or mynah bird pellets instead. Grate the kibble or pellets briefly in a blender to chop them to Lovebird size, but use the pulse speed so that you don't inadvertently reduce them to an unappetizing powder. You may offer these foods dry or mixed with a little water; your Lovebirds may find the moist version more attractive, but you shouldn't leave it out overnight.

Eggs are the most balanced and complete form of protein known, and they also offer a way to give protein that many birds find absolutely irresistible. You can make a nutritious egg-food as easily as chopping a hardboiled egg with a fork and

A Lutino Peach-faced Lovebird. A good diet will reflect itself in the bird's eyes, plumage, and overall personality.

A pair of Black-cheeked Lovebirds. Never provide natural wood perches made from trees that have been treated with dangerous chemicals.

placing it in a treat cup. Since egg can spoil rather quickly, remove the cup after about an hour.

If you'd like to leave the egg out for a full twenty-four hours, you need to mix it with something that will make it drier and more resistant to spoilage. Breeders recommend adding a teaspoonful each of brewer's yeast and powdered avian vitamins per egg to make a mix that's somewhat dry yet even more nutritious than the egg alone. Despite the assurances, however, I'm reluctant to leave this tasty mix out more than twelve hours in my hot and humid climate.

If your Lovebirds were bred by someone who offered the traditional low-protein diet, they're likely to snub their beaks at your protein offerings at first. Be patient. Continue to offer the foods you want them to try on a regular basis. If you're really concerned about the way your birds are eating, you can try removing the seed cups for an hour or two to encourage them to sample the egg mix or crumbles. But don't try to starve your birds into eating right. An underweight or hungry bird is at as much risk as an obese one.

If your Lovebird is a tame pet, it may be perfectly willing to eat a balanced diet—at least when the food's on *your* plate. If you're upset at finding a small feathered head in your plate, it's OK to give the Lovebird its own small bowl of nutritious "people" food. Small pieces of chicken or lean meat make

An American Pied Dutch Blue Peach-faced Lovebird. Grit helps the bird to grind the food in its stomach, and it also provides important trace minerals.

A pair of Fischer's Lovebirds on a natural wood perch.

great protein sources, while lightly cooked or raw vegetables and fruits are full of vitamins, fiber, and quality carbohydrates. Fresh whole grain pastas and breads are also fine. Far from hurting your bird, such table scraps will actually improve the quality of its diet.

Of course, you realize that lots of fat and sugar is no better for your bird than it is for you. It's really best if you never let your bird taste ice cream, cookies, or cake— not if you ever want to eat these treats again without avian help! However, if you offer these treats on truly rare occasions, you'll probably do no harm.

Clean water should be kept in front of your Lovebirds at all times. To prevent disease, wash out the drinker and change the water each day. Unless you're confident of the quality of your tap water—and I'm certainly not—you should probably offer distilled water to your Lovebirds. At the very least, boil the water and let it cool before offering it to your birds in order to get rid of the chlorine that can irritate birds as well as the bacteria it's designed to eliminate.

Taming & Training

It will be infinitely easier to tame your new pet if you followed my advice and chose the youngest Lovebird you possibly could. Indeed, if you've acquired a hand-fed baby, you won't have to do much taming at all. The little guy will already expect loving attention from humans.

If the Lovebird isn't tame, ask the dealer to clip its wings before you take it home. Your request is kind, not cruel, to the bird. Untamed flighted birds have been known to panic and crash into walls or other objects in their fear, sometimes breaking their necks. Since wing-clipping is painless and temporary, you will have a flighted bird again in a few weeks. At that time, your pet should be tame enough for you to clip its wings yourself if you so desire.

Let the untame Lovebird settle into its new home for a full twenty-four hours so that you can be sure it's eating well. Whenever you happen to approach the cage, talk to the bird in a low, reassuring voice to tell it that you aren't planning a sneak attack. The bird may shriek or cringe to the back of the cage at first, but its cries will become less convincing as it figures out that you mean no harm.

Once the bird's eating, you need to go ahead and start taming it. Don't put off the lessons for weeks or even months! Lovebirds grow up fast, and they base their behavior on their early training. If you don't go ahead and tame them early, you may have trouble doing it at all.

Choose a small, bird-safe area for the first lessons. A

FACING PAGE:
A Peach-faced Lovebird in flight. Before you take your pet Lovebird home from the shop, you may wish to have the dealer clip its wing. This will make the task of taming easier, since the bird will not be able to escape as easily when you start to train him.

A pair of Nyasa Lovebirds. During the period of taming and training your Lovebird, be sure to keep it separate from any other birds you may have.

bathroom tub that can be closed off from the rest of the room is a good choice. In case the bird does get out, though, be sure to lower the toilet lid, cover the mirror, and put away any fragile or poisonous items. Then you may bring a wooden stick, some treats, and the bird's cage into the training area. Close off the training area, and you're ready to begin.

Start by opening the door to the bird's cage, talking to it in a low voice all the while. Tell it what a pretty bird it is and

how much you would like to have it for a friend. Once the door is open, sit back a bit and keep talking. Let the Lovebird size up the situation. If you're lucky, it may decide to emerge from the cage on its own after a few minutes—a sign of a bird that will be a dream to train. If it's more timid, you may have to coax it out by inserting the stick into the cage and holding it at the bird's chest level. When it steps up—and parrots rarely can resist stepping up- —begin moving the stick *slowly* out of the cage. The whole time you're working, keep up a flow of reassuring words.

Once the Lovebird is on top of its cage or on the stick, you may teach it to accept treats from your hand. Offer it something special like a shelled peanut or half a fresh grape. At first it may be afraid to get so close to your hand. Be patient. Keep talking and praising it. When it does accept the treat, praise it very enthusiastically so that it will learn to associate goodies with your voice.

The next lesson involves teaching the bird to step onto your hand or finger. Some trainers advise wearing gloves because there's a chance that the frightened bird could bite. However, others point out that wearing gloves is only delaying the inevitable since sooner or later you'll still want to teach the bird to step on your ungloved hand. Unlike large parrots, most Lovebirds probably haven't had any terrifying experiences with gloves, so this step most likely won't actively harm your growing relationship with your pet. However, it's an extra step you don't have to take unless you're really nervous. It may help to remember that although a Lovebird bite can be painful, it won't really damage you.

Gloved or not, you should move your hand up to the Lovebird's chest very slowly, talking all the time so it knows you're not trying to come in for a sneaky grab. When it decides to step up, it will probably lower its beak to steady itself on its new perch. This steadying action with the beak won't hurt you, so don't yank away and frustrate your pet. Let it see that you represent a safe, comfortable place to be.

If the bird does bite, simply say "no" in a loud voice and continue with the lesson. Never hit or punish a bird. It won't learn anything from punishment except to fear you—and that's the last thing you want.

Once the bird's on your finger, you can offer it another treat, praise it to the skies, and let it eat from your hand with your proud words singing in its ears. When it's finished eating, you should check your watch to make sure the lesson hasn't gone on too long. Even a young, healthy bird shouldn't be worked for more than twenty or thirty minutes. Gently return the bird to its cage and plan on continuing the training after not less than an hour and more than a day has passed.

Next time, you can help your Lovebird learn to step from hand to hand. Praise it each time it responds quickly. Don't be afraid to show your enthusiasm. You can't feed it every time it does the right thing or it would soon be full to bursting, but you can certainly shower it with kind words. After a time, it will become trusting enough to walk up to your shoulder or head. Discourage it from using the head as a perch, please. A loud "no" and removing the bird to the shoulder should do the trick.

Once a bird trusts you and actively clamors to leave its cage to ride your shoulder, it's tame. However, you can make both your lives a little easier if you insist on one more step— teaching the bird to accept your hand around its body or on its

A rare Black-winged Lovebird in a show cage. This bird has obviously had a successful show career.

Taming and Training Your Lovebird

A pair of Masked Lovebirds. Lovebirds need attention; if you do not have the necessary time to tame and train your pet, be sure to provide it with a companion.

head. You must work very slowly and carefully when you first start scratching your Lovebird's head. Move *very* gradually as you rub its ears. After a few lessons, it will realize that it loves being scratched and it may "bop" your hand with its head to get you to scratch it. Great! After awhile, you will be able to cup your hand over the bird's head and even over its back, petting it very gently. Although the bird may never be 100% thrilled about having you wrap your hand over it, you will be glad you taught it to tolerate this handling every time you must clip its nails or hold it for the vet.

Once it's tame and confident of your kindness, the Lovebird may sometimes seem to be taking advantage of you. Parrot owners usually have to cope with two major problems—screaming and biting. If your Lovebird shrieks a greeting when you get home, I wouldn't be concerned. It's just saying hello. If it constantly shrieks for attention, however, something's

wrong. Are you spending enough time with it? Fifteen or twenty minutes a day may satisfy an independent Amazon, but a single Lovebird needs more affection than that. Build a playpen so it can travel about the house with you as you do your chores. Set out its own small plate so it can share your dinner. Let it join you during TV. You'll soon find that it's easier than you think to give your Lovebird the hours of affection it demands.

Of course, if you've done all that and it's still complaining, the Lovebird may be trying to "guilt-trip" you into letting it run the household. In that case, place it in its cage and cover it up when it shrieks. Besides shutting it up at once—few birds care to scream in the dark—this treatment will teach it that shrieking isn't the way to win attention.

Young Lovebirds, particularly Peach-faced Lovebirds, often go through a teething phase when they seem to bite or chew everything in sight. Tell them "no" in a loud, firm voice when they bite or chew something they shouldn't, then direct them to something they *can* exercise their little beaks on. The habit should eventually pass.

Once your Lovebird is tame, you may want to teach it some tricks. Great! These intelligent little birds often welcome the chance to learn new ways of winning human attention. Although it's rare in these relatively nonvocal parrots, a few Lovebirds even learn to talk.

When working with untame adult Lovebirds or even tame pets, professional trainers often use a food reward to teach tricks. While the technique works very well, it takes time and patience. Every step of the way, you must offer the Lovebird a treat, quickly filling it up. The lessons don't go very far in any one session, so it can take quite a while to teach a trick.

However, once you have a good relationship with your pet Lovebird, you can reward it with something that will never fill it up—affection and attention. You can scratch its head, shower it with praise, and generally reward it with making it the center of your attention. Your pet will love it. In fact, affection-trained birds have the greatest chance of becoming avian "hams" that welcome the chance to show off for humans.

Besides giving your Lovebird another way to win your

Artist's rendering of a Peach-faced Lovebird.

attention, training helps encourage the bird to exercise. Remember, a wild Lovebird might fly for miles in search of food. A little trick-training can encourage your sedentary pet to give his heart and muscles a healthy workout.

It's easiest to teach tricks that are based on the Lovebird's natural behaviors. For instance, you can easily teach your pet to play "tug of war" with a piece of cardboard or chain. It's fun to tug gently and feel your small bird respond with surprising strength. Other easy tricks take advantage of your Lovebird's curiosity about its toys. Teach it to climb a ladder or ring a bell on command by setting up the toy on its playpen, asking the bird to "Climb the ladder" or "Ring the bell." When it does so, praise it profusely. With time, it will associate the command with the activity and know what it must do to win praise. At that point, your bird will perform on command!

There's a variety of toys and props offered through stores and pet bird magazines for training your bird to try even more ambitious tricks. Want to teach your Lovebird to ride a scooter or drop a coin in a piggy bank? The props are out there.

Never forget that training your bird should be fun, not a struggle. A Lovebird's attention span is short, and it should not be asked to work on a trick for longer than ten or twenty minutes at a time. Be patient, gentle, and lavish with praise, and always try to end each session on an "up" note. If the bird has mastered something new within the first five minutes of the session, great! Praise the bird and give it a treat before you move on. There are no prizes for "fastest trained bird."

I will describe how you can teach your Lovebird to talk for the benefit of those of you with a lot of patience. However, don't make your love for the bird dependent on its ability to talk. Lovebirds are intelligent, but they just aren't very gifted vocalists. If you really crave a talking bird, it's better to buy a Budgerigar or one of the Amazon parrots. Your very best chance of getting a talking Lovebird is to buy a hand-fed youngster that has already picked up a few words from its breeder—if the breeder can be convinced to part with such a splendid bird!

Don't waste your time trying to teach an adult Lovebird to talk. The younger the bird is when you start its training, the more of a chance you'll have of coaxing a few words out of it. You also have a better chance of teaching it to talk if you work at home, where you can expose it to your chitchat at all hours of the day.

Formal lessons should take place for five minutes at a time at least once a day and preferably several times a day. Get the Lovebird on your finger, hold it up where you can look at each other, and repeat the phrase you'd like it to learn. Start with something short but distinctive, like "pretty bird." Repeat the phrase over and over in a firm, clear, but cheerful voice.

It's a good idea to supplement personal lessons by playing an endless loop cassette with the phrase recorded on it.

Taming and Training Your Lovebird

A pair of normally colored Peach-faced Lovebirds. Before placing two Lovebirds in the same area, be sure they are compatible.

That way, the Lovebird can be practicing while you're gone so that you won't go bananas before it has learned its first word. However, it isn't a good idea to let the cassette play for eight hours at a stretch because the bird will simply learn to "tune out" the phrase. Play it for more like twenty minutes or perhaps an hour when you're out on an errand. Good luck!.

43

Breeding

Breeding Lovebirds is a hobby that can be adapted to almost anyone's level of skill and interest. These birds have such a strong drive to reproduce that even a beginner with just a pair or two in moderately sized cages can enjoy success. Yet, because there are so many exciting new mutations being developed and a few rare Lovebirds that need to be better established in captivity, an expert breeder can find Lovebird breeding a life-long challenge. Furthermore, breeding the birds yourself is the number one way to get a real "peach" of a pet. And, once you're hand-rearing Lovebirds, don't be surprised if you must establish a waiting list for all the people eager to buy your sweethearts.

We mentioned earlier that the toughest part of breeding Lovebirds can be making sure you have a true pair, since the sexes look alike in the most popular species of Lovebirds. Here's where the person who intends to devote a lot of space to Lovebirds has an advantage over the hobbyist who can only start with one pair. If you have several Lovebirds to examine, it becomes easier to sex them if only by comparison. With several birds sitting side by side, it's easier to pick out the slightly heavier females or to feel which birds have the most distinct spacing between their pelvic bones. So, even if you plan to set up your pairs in individual cages, you will have a better chance of establishing some true pairs than the person who just bought the last two Lovebirds left in the store.

We also mentioned that Peach-faced Lovebirds and the four species with white eyerings are adapted to breeding in colonies. Since you're probably starting with one of these popular species, you could also place your birds in a colony aviary so

A pair of Dutch Blue Peach-faced Lovebirds. The first step toward breeding Lovebirds is finding a genetically and temperamentally suited breeding pair.

that they can choose their own mates. They tend to like that better, since Lovebirds don't necessarily want to accept the mate you choose for them. However, the rare and timid woodland Lovebirds, such as the Grey-headed, Black-winged, and Red-faced Lovebirds, shouldn't be asked to breed in colonies since they naturally breed in widely separated territories and could be too territorial to share space with other pairs. Fortunately, the males and females of these species do look different, so that you won't run into any problem pairing them off should you encounter these rarities.

However, if you simply don't have room for more than a pair or two of Lovebirds, don't despair. At about eight months to a year old, you may start encouraging the birds to breed by giving them special food, nesting material, and so on. Since the common Lovebirds rarely need much urging to go to nest, you can watch and see what happens. Are the birds working hard to build a nest which they proceed to fill up with eight or ten eggs? You've got two hens. Are they mating but then just sitting there looking at each other, waiting for the other to get to work? You probably have two males (although there's an off chance that you have a female who is in poor condition or just not ready to lay). Find someone else—perhaps through your pet store or a bird club—who's in a similar situation and arrange a swap. Sometimes a bird specialty store will allow you to swap one of your birds until you have a true pair. It never hurts to ask.

Since the popular Lovebirds can be bred in cages or colonies, perhaps you're wondering which method is better. That really depends on you and your goals. Each method has its advantages and disadvantages. It's up to you to pick the technique that helps you breed the birds you want.

Naturally, if you've just got a pair or two, you'll probably breed them in a cage. Yet, are you surprised to learn that many top breeders also breed their Lovebirds in cages? It's true. Cage-breeding offers a number of powerful advantages for someone who dreams of raising show quality birds or birds with special colors. When you set up Lovebirds in cages, you get to say who breeds to whom, thus encouraging the development of particular bloodlines. It's really the only method if you

A Masked Lovebird hen incubating her eggs inside the nestbox.

have your heart set on developing a new color mutation.

On the other hand, if you prefer Lovebirds who look and behave more like they would in the wild, you will probably want to consider colony breeding. In this situation, you have relatively little control over who mates with whom, so special color mutations tend to get swamped. But, since normal-colored Lovebirds do tend to be the hardiest specimens, you may consider that just as well.

Whatever you decide, try not to encourage your Lovebirds to breed too young. They may look like adults at four months, but let them mature a little before coaxing them to breed. Lovebirds have a potential lifespan of some twelve to sixteen years, so there's really no great rush. In fact, your hen will probably live longer and stay healthier if you let her put a little meat on her bones before asking her to lay. I realize that these determined little birds may not always wait for your permission to get started, but do the best you can to build up their systems before urging them to barrel forward full steam ahead.

When you're ready to give the birds a nudge, be sure to review their diets. Do they have unlimited access to a fresh, clean source of calcium such as a cuttlebone or mineral block? Are you giving—and are the birds eating—a good source of protein at least every other day? Is there an adequate supply of vitamins A, D, and E in the diet? It's so easy to let the quality of the diet slip after those first few months of beginner's dedication, but your birds will stay in better condition if you don't succumb to the temptation.

You can often encourage indoor birds to start breeding by placing a timer on the light source. To fool the birds into thinking it's spring, you can gradually build up the lighting to about fourteen hours a day. However, you may not need to bother with this technique unless your pairs really seem reluctant to get started. The resilient Lovebird can be so indifferent to weather that there are reports of colonies breeding outdoors in winter—in Britain! Although the youngsters will probably be just fine in their snug, well-lined nests, it's wise to supply a heat lamp so that hens about to lay can warm up first and relax their muscles if they need to.

Most parrots do little or no fussing over the nest. Not the Lovebirds. They snub their little beaks at the very idea of nesting on the bare floor of a Budgie nestbox. Instead, they will build a snug nest of their own inside the box. Their desire for a homey nest is so strong that they will pluck their own or another's feathers for material if enough isn't forthcoming. (For that matter, they may pluck their own or another's feathers for material *anyway*.) You can offer an assortment of clean materials for your Lovebirds to build with: willow leaves and branches, palm fronds, sterilized duck or goose down, sterilized goat hair, even the generic "nesting material" offered by the pet shop. Willow is probably the Lovebird's favorite construction material, so do try to offer some if it's at all possible. Make sure that whatever you offer is clean and mite-free so that the little ones won't start their lives with a permanent itch.

If you can sit quietly and watch your Lovebirds work on the nest, do so. It's an amusing sight. The male will probably

A pair of Peach-faced Lovebirds. Before breeding any Lovebirds, be sure that both birds are in excellent physical condition.

help shred the nest material and he may even want to help with the actual building, but the sturdier female will do all of the real work. The Peach-faced Lovebird hen will stuff the nesting material among her rump feathers before carrying it to the nest, often letting the material stream behind her like the tail of a kite. The popular Lovebirds with eyerings will carry the nesting materials in their bill, but the rarer woodland Lovebirds will also stuff nesting material among their feathers. They may drop a lot along the way, but their enthusiasm never falters.

Sometimes what you'll see is two Lovebirds fighting, fussing, and feather-plucking instead of working together in happy harmony. In that case, act quickly, since a Lovebird is capable of hurting or killing a mate it doesn't care for. Split the birds up for several days, then try them together again. Often the brief vacation is all they need to decide that the other bird's OK after all. However, if the birds continue to quarrel, you may have to split them up for good.

You probably won't have to worry about incompatibility problems in a colony aviary if you're careful. After the Lovebirds have paired off, you can remove any leftover birds for sale or care in individual cages. To prevent squabbles between pairs, always provide one-and-a-half to two nestboxes per pair. You should also have a feeder for every four birds or so, especially if some of your Lovebirds are the bossy types who try to chase others from the bowl.

Expect the hen to lay three to five eggs. She will usually be the one who incubates them, although her mate may sit with her. The youngsters will start hatching after twenty-two to twenty-five days. If your Lovebirds are calm birds like the Peach-faced, you can establish a routine of opening the nestbox each day to check on the progress of eggs and young. Try to make your inspection at about the same time every day, preferably when the adults are off the nest. Remember that, although tame Lovebirds probably won't be frightened by your interference, their tempers could become extremely short. In other words, be careful where you poke your fingers if you don't want a Lovebird beak sunk into them. Nervous Lovebirds will probably do better if you skip the inspections. Expect the youngsters to start venturing from the nest at around forty days after hatch, give or take a few days.

If you notice a hen with a swollen vent who's squatting on the floor of the cage or obviously straining to pass an egg, you have an eggbound hen. You must act at once, because the hen's life is at stake. If she's already in a small cage, clip a lamp near one end for warmth and see if the extra heat relaxes her enough to let her pass the egg. If she doesn't expel it in two

Peach-faced Lovebirds outside a typical nestbox. If you plan to breed a number of Lovebirds, be sure to have a sufficient amount of nestboxes.

or three hours, you must take more drastic action.

Before capturing her, bring a pot of water to a rolling boil on the stove and then turn off the heat. Then pick up the eggbound hen in a dry towel and hold her over the warm steam. (Make sure it's cooled enough not to scald!) You may also dab a *tiny* amount of petroleum jelly on her vent to ease the egg's passage. If the steam and jelly don't work, take her to the vet immediately. Eggbinding is a true emergency, because if the hen doesn't pass the egg within a reasonable amount of time or if the egg breaks within her, she will certainly die. Unless you're under the supervision of a vet or other expert, never try to massage an eggbound hen's belly in an attempt to make her expel the egg; chances are too high that inexperienced hands would simple break the egg inside her.

Since eggbinding is usually caused by a nutritional deficiency, you should beef up the diet of all your breeding Lovebirds right away. Have you been mixing vitamins A and D in the seed? Are there enough cuttlebones for everyone in the aviary? Sometimes, of course, the hen gets egghound because she was really too young to breed and her body hadn't had time to stockpile enough nutrients for the task. All you can do about that is to continue to discourage younger Lovebirds from breeding and accept the fact that you won't always succeed.

If all goes well, expect 75% to 80% of your fertile eggs to hatch. If your hatchability rate is lower, take another look at your breeding set-up. Did the developing chicks die in the shell because they didn't have enough protein to keep growing? Next time, make sure the hen gets plenty of protein food before she starts laying. If she isn't eating the protein food you offer, try something else. Did the parents toss the eggs out of the nest to die? If the Lovebirds are inexperienced, they could just be suffering from first-time nerves. Let them try again. If they're older, maybe you bothered them too much or they didn't feel they had enough protein food to raise healthy young.

A big problem that prevents successful hatches in Lovebirds is low humidity. I think it's too risky for a beginner to try misting the nest or placing soaked moss in the nest box, as some Lovebird experts do. How is the beginner to know how much humidity is too much? Drowned eggs won't hatch any better than dried out ones. Fortunately, you do have someone right there with you who knows exactly how much humidity the eggs need—the birds themselves. Give them a dog dish or another type of bathing dish full of clean water each day, and they will splash and soak their feathers until the humidity is just right.

FACING PAGE:
A pair of dark factor Peach-faced Lovebirds. The
many color combinations present in Lovebird
genetics makes breeding a challenge to the
experienced as well as to the novice.

Species and Mutations

Between the nine species of Lovebirds and the many varieties of some of these species being developed by breeders, Lovebirds offer a range of colors, habits, and personality characteristics. But before you can understand the possibilities, you have to know a little about the difference between species, subspecies, and mutations.

A species is a group of animals that can and will breed freely and produce fertile young in the wild. For example, although a Peach-faced Lovebird and a Fischer's Lovebird can mate and produce fertile young in captivity, they're members of different species because they would not do so in the wild. A subspecies occurs when members of a species become separated into two or more groups for so long that the two groups begin to look a little different. The change in an individual's genetic code that causes it to look different is called a mutation. Notice that a mutation is a change that occurs *within* a true species. It is not the result of breeding birds from two different species, something that rarely occurs in the wild.

In order to preserve the genetic heritage of each species, most Lovebird breeders advise against mating members of two different species, since hybridizing just produces "mongrels" who can't be allowed to reproduce. If you're interested in creating new mutations of Lovebirds, you will work within a single species—often within a single family bloodline—in order to concentrate the characteristics you want to develop. Your work will take skill and planning, because inbreeding to create mutations can concentrate bad characteristics as well as good ones. To learn more about genetics and breeding Lovebird mutations, consult one of the fine books available on the subject to help you get started.

The nine species of Lovebirds represent two distinct groups: the species with white eyerings that breed in colonies, and the sexually dimorphic group that lacks the eyerings and

LEFT: A pair of Black-cheeked Lovebirds. RIGHT: A lovely yellow mutation of Fischer's Lovebird.

breeds in widely separated territories. The Peach-faced Lovebird, which lacks an eyering but also breeds in colonies, represents an intermediate stage between the two groups. There is also a rare species called the Black-collared Lovebird that we know little about.

The Eyering Species

Since they're so closely related and can interbreed so freely, some people have argued that the four species of eyering Lovebirds should actually be reclassified as one species. Observers have reported seeing Fischer's and Masked Lovebirds flocking together in the wild, and the care and habits of all four species are very similar. Whether they represent four true species or just four subspecies, they'll definitely interbreed in captive colonies. To prevent the destruction of the natural forms, never keep mixed colonies of these birds or they may opt to interbreed on their own.

The Masked Lovebird (*Agapornis personata*) is a very popular species that's available in a number of attractive mutations. They originally came from an inland plateau, where their wild counterparts range through forested grasslands foraging among seeding grasses and shrubs. Intelligent, alert, and self-confident, the Masked Lovebird is surpassed in popularity only by the exquisitely colored Peach-faced.

When breeding Masked Lovebirds, be sure to supply them with all the willow branches and bath water they need. Masks go in for some intricate nest-building, sometimes producing such elaborate interiors that breeders have been surprised by "extra" fledglings that had really been concealed in a secret tunnel in the nest. Their eggs and young seem to thrive at a fairly high humidity, so don't worry if they seem to dunk a lot of material in their bath dish before placing it in the nest.

The normal Mask is a mostly green bird with a wide collar of yellow around its neck and a brownish-black head that looks to me more like a dark hood than a mask. The first and most common mutation is the Blue-masked, which is also known to occur in the wild. Despite the name, this lovely bird doesn't have a blue mask; its head is still black, but the green areas on the normal have been replaced with blue, while the yellow areas have been replaced with white.

Other fairly common mutations are the Yellow-masked, which has the normally green areas replaced with a mottled yellow-green, and the White-masked, which is a paler version of the Blue-masked. More unusual are the Albinos, with pure white feathers, and the Lutinos, yellow birds with pinkish masks.

Another popular species of eyering Lovebirds is Fischer's Lovebirds (*A. fischeri*). They live in habitat similar to the Masked Lovebird's, although they seldom meet Masks in the wild. Because they like seeding grasses, they will feed on cultivated millet and other grain when they can. They often nest among the bases of palm fronds and in captivity enjoy re-

LEFT: A Nyasa Lovebird. RIGHT: An American Pied Light Green Peach-faced Lovebird. This is one of the most popular color varieties among Lovebird breeders today.

ceiving palm fronds that they can shred for nesting material.

The normal Fischer's is mostly green, with a reddish-orange face and throat. Any beginner not sure how "reddish-orange" differs from "peach" can distinguish them from Peach-faced Lovebirds by looking for the white eyering. Since fewer breeders are developing mutations of Fischer's, the Yellow, Lutino, and Blue Fischer's are quite rare, and the individual with the interest and resources to develop a line of these birds can expect to be handsomely rewarded.

Black-cheeked Lovebirds (*A. nigrigenis*) have the smallest range of any Lovebird. Because they were trapped to the point of extinction in the 1920s, their export was banned in

1929. Since they were rarely bred—and sometimes hybridized with other Lovebirds when they were—they remain rather rare in captivity.

The Black-cheeked Lovebird is mostly green, with a dark brown forehead, black cheeks and throat, and a crescent of pale orange-red on its upper breast. In the past, breeders offered a blue "mutation" which was not a mutation at all but a hybrid with the Blue-masked Lovebird. Don't buy such hybrids, or you will be encouraging the production of an artificial form at the expense of a true species.

The Nyasa Lovebird (*A. lilianae*) looks much like a Black-cheeked with an orange face, cheeks, crown, and throat. Beginners can avoid confusing them with Peach-faced Lovebirds by looking for the Nyasa's white eyering, and they can distinguish them from Fischer's Lovebird by looking for the latter bird's stripe of yellow across the breast. In the wild, they prefer to stick to river valleys, but otherwise their behavior is much like that of the other eyering species.

A trio of Black-winged Lovebirds. The male is the bird with the red patch on its forehead.

LEFT: A male Red-faced Lovebird. RIGHT: A male Grey-headed Lovebird.

Nyasa Lovebirds can be prolific breeders when kept in a large colony. Consequently, a few breeders have tried to develop some Nyasa mutations. The Lutino version, a golden-yellow bird with white flight feathers and an orange head, is considered quite beautiful but is also extremely rare.

Peach-faced Lovebirds

Peach-faced Lovebirds (*A. roseicollis*) are by far the most popular species of Lovebirds. These intelligent, attractive birds are plentiful in their range throughout the arid grasslands of southwest Africa. Adaptable and gregarious, breeding colonies often steal the intricately woven nests of weaver birds for their own. However, they only rob as many nests as they need, leaving the rest for the weavers. Alternatively, they will nest in the ridges of cliffs or the crevices of buildings.

Normal peachies are green birds with peach-colored faces and throats. There is, of course, no eyering around the dark, mischievous eye. Semi-tame or untame adults are usually eager to breed, while hand-fed peachies make affectionate and intelligent pets. They're a great choice for someone who wants to start breeding birds with a sturdy, enthusiastic species that won't let minor mistakes prevent it from producing young.

There are many, many mutations of these popular birds. Pied birds possess patches of different colors in unexpected areas so that no two Pied birds will look exactly alike. The Lutino Peach-faced, said by many to be the most beautiful Lovebird, is golden-yellow with a peachie face. Since hens are dubious about the little red Lutino babies, often refusing to feed them or even mutilating them, it's wise to hand-rear these special youngsters if you possibly can. Other mutations include various shades of blue peachies with white faces, albinos, "cream-inos," olive, cinnamon, and many others. If you'd like to learn more about Peach-faced mutations, consult an advanced book like *The World of Lovebirds* by Jurgen Brockmann and Werner Lantermann. If you're more interested in getting a single pet, choose your Lovebird for personality first and color second. A hand-fed "lover" will soon convince you it's the prettiest one of all!

The Sexually Dimorphic Lovebirds

The three species of sexually dimorphic Lovebirds are shy birds that should be bred in individual flights or cages. Since they're relatively rare, anyone who owns these birds should consider breeding them rather than taming them as pets. A beginner is unlikely to run across any of these species, but they're something to dream about if you get deeply into Lovebird breeding.

The Grey-headed or Madagascar Lovebird (*A. cana*) is a small green Lovebird. Only the males have the gray heads, while the females are green all over. They are nervous birds

A Fischer's Lovebird in a natural setting. Fischer's Lovebirds are very similar to some varieties of Masked Lovebirds.

who should be given a cozy nestbox and a quiet place to breed without much interference from the breeder or the curious.

The male Red-faced Lovebird (*A. pullaria*) is a green bird with a red face. The female's face is a paler orange. You can also sex them by checking under the wing coverts (the part of the wing nearest the body); males have black under their wing coverts while females have green. In the wild, these birds nest in tree termite mounds, and wild-caught birds must be tricked into going to nest with elaborate nestboxes that simulate the conditions in an arboreal termitary. Fortunately, captive-bred birds have learned to accept more traditional nestboxes.

The Abyssinian or Black-winged Lovebird (*A. taranta*) is green with black flight feathers. The males have red foreheads, while the females have all-green heads. As with the other members of this group, they need a private flight where they can breed without disturbance.

An Enigmatic Lovebird

Very little is known about the Black-collared Lovebird (*A. swinderniana*), which can be identified by the neat black collar on the back of its neck. Both sexes look alike, and their nesting habits are pretty much unknown, although it's thought that they may nest in arboreal termitaries like the Red-faced Lovebird. They haven't been imported because it's believed that they can't survive without a special kind of wild fig that grows in their homeland. Whether that's truth or just speculation, I can't say, but one thing's for sure: once you start with Lovebirds, you'll never run out of opportunities for mystery and delight.

Suggested Reading

The following books by T.F.H. Publications are available at pet shops everywhere.

ALL ABOUT BREEDING LOVEBIRDS
By Mervin F. Roberts
ISBN 0-87666-943-7
T.F.H. PS-800
This book will be especially valuable for the many lovebird fanciers, beginners and experienced aviculturists alike.
Hard cover, 5½ x 8"; 96 pages
Cóntains full-color and black and white photos

HANDBOOK OF LOVEBIRDS
By Horst Bielfield
with a special section on
DISEASES OF PARROTS
By Dr. Manfred Heidenreich
ISBN 0-87666-820-1
TFH H-1040
For the aviculturist specializing in lovebirds and owners of parrots of any size. Of interest to novice bird-keepers as well as advanced fanciers. Comprehensive; contains special section on the diseases of parrots useful to all parrot owners, not just lovebirds.
Hard cover, 8½ x 11", 111 pages, 117 full-color photos, 10 b/w photos.

LOVEBIRDS: A Complete Introduction
By Georg A. Radtke
Hardcvr **CO-030 ISBN 0-86622-365-7 $7.95**
Softcvr **CO-030S ISBN 0-86622-382-7 $4.95**
This book has the most comprehensive coverage for the beginner as well as the advanced hobbyist. Written by one of the world's leading authorities on lovebirds, this easy-to-read book covers all of the topics of importance: selection, accommodations, diet, breeding and illness.
5½ x 8½", 96 pages
Contains 74 full-color photos and 28 full-color line drawings.

Index